A Casserole Of Kisses

Samuel Onyeche

Shantel Awajionyi Igana

Ukiyoto Publishing

All global publishing rights are held by

Ukiyoto Publishing

Published in 2023

Content Copyright ©
Samuel Onyeche & Shantel Awajionye Igana

ISBN 9789360161200

*All rights reserved.
No part of this publication may be reproduced,
transmitted, or stored in a retrieval system, in any
form by any means, electronic, mechanical,
photocopying, recording or otherwise, without the
prior permission of the publisher.*

The moral rights of the author have been asserted.

*This is a work of fiction. Names, characters,
businesses, places, events, locales, and incidents are
either the products of the author's imagination or used
in a fictitious manner. Any resemblance to actual
persons, living or dead, or actual events is purely
coincidental.*

*This book is sold subject to the condition that it shall
not by way of trade or otherwise, be lent, resold, hired
out or otherwise circulated, without the publisher's
prior consent, in any form of binding or cover other
than that in which it is published.*

This book is dedicated to you, our dear reader.

Acknowledgements

The birth of this beautiful brain-child wouldn't have been possible without the inspiration, strength and provision of the Almighty God. May Him alone be glorified. I say a big thank you to my wonderful parents Mr and Mrs Jonathan Alozie Onyeche and to my ever supportive sister Joy Chidinma Tochuwkwu I'm so blessed to have you in my life.

My unreserved gratitude goes to the following digniteries , Prof. Kontein Trinya, Prof. Samuel Otamiri, Prof. Samuel Amaele , Dr Anthony Orlu, Dr Wellington Nwogu, John Chinaka Onyeche, Goodness Obinnah, and poet Shantel Awajionyi Igana, I am forever indebted to these Angels in human form. (Samuel A. Onyeche.)

My unfeigned recognition goes to God Almighty for His imposing mercy and devoted love. I also with an obliged heart appreciate my one-in-a-kind biological father, Chief. I. S. Ikpogo for his incessant drudgery to make me expressive. I am indebted. I cannot forget these material persons in my life, Awaji-Imam Igoni, Adedayo John Abimbade, Poet Samuel Alozie Onyeche, Pst. I. G. Zalmon.God bless your efforts. (Shantel Awajionyi Igana)

About the Book

If you are a fruit
I will give you no name
Cause the real things of life are unnamed
I will plant you beside my bank
Encircled with lilies
And grasped my breath from your every spring.

A CASSEROLE OF KISSES is a co-authored poetry collection with deep lyrical enchantments and winepress stanzas that resplendently appeal to both the mind and soul, It holds pages of beautiful expressions of love, emotional mysteries, and its attendant pang. This book is an embodiment of wit, refined aesthetics and didacticism crafted to entertain, inspire and educate its readers on matters of love and romance.
A casserole of kisses; a scintillating blend of sweetness and beauty wrapped into one alluring collection.
Edidiong Etukudoh: Lawyer and Poet.

The poets show profundity in their choice of words and in the arrangements of their carefully chosen words which are capable of mesmerising any reader.

Nathaniel Okeke
A Multiple Award Winning Poet & President, Nigerian Young Writers Association

Poets are master keys opening doors
to deep thinks, to deep things and realities.

-Edidiong Etukudoh
Lawyer & Poet

Contents

Poems By Shantel Awajionyi Igana   1
Poems By Samuel Onyeche   50

About the Authors   *84*

Foreword

It was T. S. Elliot who wrote, 'words are not enough to say to you how much I love you.' He further said, "It is obvious that we can no more explain a passion to a person who has never experienced it than we can explain light to the blind. But it should be obvious also that we can explain the passion equally well: it is no more 'subjective', because some persons have never experienced it, than light is subjective because the blind cannot see."

Indeed, words are not enough, but since a lover must write and love birds must sing, these poets have carefully woven these lines in this beautiful collection you are holding. In 'A Casserole of Kisses', the poets write with punch, in addition to the relative metaphors used in making the anthology a compact read. In this thriller, the duo do not only attempt to explain light to the blind but are also able to make the blind to crave for light. One of the most magical things that a person can do to another is to make him hunger for what he would ordinarily ignore. Even though no one may claim to be ignoring love, the poets make us to understand that one can never get enough of it. They succeeded in making a blind man beg his 'Chi' to give him light.

If I say that this collection is one that is capable of making even the most unlovable persons to fall in love, the readers may think that I am deliberately exaggerating, but I trust that any reader who picks this collection to read, would not only agree with me on what I said, but would find out more beautiful reasons to agree as they will be held spellbound while reading the poems in this anthology.

I have read quite a number of poetry collections on love and romance, but I can beat my chest to say that this collection is unique and outstanding. The theme of love is handled carefully, critically and poetically.

One thing that is consistent in this collection is the figurative disposition and the ability of the poets to creatively employ metaphysical elements in their poetry. Every poem in this collection has a unique element that defines love in such a way that the reader is held up in such a rhapsodic and rapturous curiosity to read on. Metaphysical poems have the elements of metaphors, metaphysical conceits, paradoxes, and analogies. Metaphors and metaphysical conceits, a type of extended metaphor which are used to show a connection between two things that are not similar and to prove the speaker's point in his poem. So, not only do the speakers in the various poems use metaphysical elements, but employ other suiting devices to make the poems rich.

The metaphors and other figurative languages are beyond the ordinary. Without an external aid, one is able to read and assign accurate meanings to the poems which makes them stuff for every lovelorn.

The poems recount sacrifices that are expected of those who must become cowards for the sake of love. Beyond the literariness of the collection, there are hidden messages buried in each piece. The sacredness of love and the enthralling and entangling hands it has which it uses to grasp not just the heart of the lover, but the entirety of the one who claims to love.

The poets show profundity in their choice of words and in the arrangements of their carefully chosen words which are capable of mesmerising any reader. A lot of poets have written on theme of love and romance, but not many have carefully combined the elements of the metaphysical to dish out such beautiful poems.

A lot of writers fail to acknowledge the fact that in every love song, the heart must be faster than the lips and so must the head. Now that we have found them in this collection, we must acknowledge them.

Nathaniel Okeke
A Multiple Award Winning Poet & President, Nigerian Young Writers Association

Poems by
Shantel Awajionyi Igana

A Casserole Of Kisses

How does love taste?

Is it like honey that sours after many waters?

Or like four feet on a futon; relating, and after awhile; dim?

I have dined on many tables; but, your love is a living bread;

never to hunger

I have drank; from many oceans; but, your kisses are living waters

Never thirst again; Flowing on to eternity

Victoria,

Your love is a lamb; you thrill me in your ways

And I blush like a cow

Your love smells like lychees and it, my fragrance is

Who will rescue me from these gross yearnings?

None should rescue me; let me perish in this promised land

For crowns await every trimmer

But firstly, love will clap for me
Your love is like a garden on sunny days
Your love is like a freshly ripped blackberry
I will eternally be a faithful harvester

Victoria,
I want to colour your colours on colours
And make rainbows envious,
I want to write your righteousness on the wind's back
And make the angels wonder,
I want to love you more,
Drunk in your wine
And sleep on.,
I want to stumble as angels
And rue as humans
For everything there's a season
So let me plant my Eden
In your heart
Where only bouquets and I grow

Fair Victoria,
Is love not a mortal
With parts and blood?
If I am pricked, won't I bleed?
So my love is immorality
Never a prick will I bleed
Cause every drop of my clot is
An utter lost of you
Your love is greedy and I am privileged
Live on in me; your license expires
When we part no more

Victoria, My Victoria,
Receive my casserole of kisses
Envied by undeserved eyes
But my presence shall your armour be
For I have built around you, towers,
Surrounded with helmets; with my love
And set tables roundabout you; with my promises
I have mounted thousand soldiers on your gates; with my eyes
Receive my casserole of kisses; till time ticks no more

Because Of You

Because of you,
I laughed hard like a remco toy
I smiled far-reaching like an ultraviolet light
With my cauliflower teeth colouring the night

Because of you,
I misspelt my name
When competing with the Pillars of Creation
Cause your fondness stone-blind my sobriety

Because of you,
I missed many paths to early demise
When cessation called my fainted soul
When sufferance kitted me with wails
When life played keen pranks on me

Because of you
Warm fuzzies erected a castle in my being
Assembled hundreds of butterflies in my solar plexus
Spinning, spinning and spinning
With lingering laughter stretching my looks

Because of you,

Because of you,

Because of you!

I will defile death a million times

to live in this rapture

You Are The Replica Of My Laughter

As brave as a tempest
As jovial as a cricket
As flexible as a feather
So is my laughter

As innocent as a toddler
As durable as a moniker
As soft as fur, so is my laughter
And you are the replica of my laughter

As safe as holy houses
Like a jaki driver on horses
Is my laughter, as easy as a pie
Straight as a die

Still, as instrumental as a tool
As neat as a pool
Is my laughter
And you are the replica of this laughter

As satisfactory as water
As cool as cucumber
As concerned as a mother
So is my lasting laughter

My laughter is as drunk as a lord
My love, come fill my heart like God
For you are so rare; as rare as gold
With or without wealth, we shall forever grow old

I Am Accused

I am accused
Of dancing naked
In my apparel

I am accused
Of laughing aloud
When nothing amuses me
I am accused
Of madness
In my sanity

I am accused
Of clapping for the giggling blueberries
At night
And at noon

I am accused
Of forsaking beautiful dairies
For stars of the morning
They tarry not

I am accused
Of being handcuffed
By the songs of Solomon
Where solos moan

I am accused
Of crooning lullabies for adults
And hovering droplets of rain on babies
Mercilessly,

I am accused
And found guilty
Of affection
For a being I knew
But never saw

I am accused
Of watering the gardens
With silly smiles
Who has made her mad?

Nothing Is As Perfect As You

Nothing is sweeter
than the kisses of honey
Nothing is scarcer
than the diamonds of gold

Nothing is terrible
as angry army with death in their hands
Nothing is brighter
than the eyes of a silver sun

Nothing is as beautiful
as the skin of roses
Nothing is as safe
as the cocoon of heaven

Nothing is as splashy
as the smile of a female rainbow
Nothing is as concerned
as the heart of a mother

Enyina, as nothing
is as enduring as true love
So nothing is as perfect
as you

Arikemi

I will enthrone you
On the cathedra of eternities
For your love is like the balm of Gilead
It soothes my forlornness
I will build your tentacles
In my existence
Your gentle touches
Encompasses me like a
Mother's chest over her bairn
I will paint your name
On the glossy faces of the firmaments
For you worth more than rubies

Arikemi

I will telegraph your beauty all over the cosmos
With drums
With Sekere
With Udu
With Agidigbo
With Gangan
With Ekwe
Even your qualities, in my <u>race</u>
Devoid of partition
I will dance with you, along countless feet
Not with brass neither string
But with bamboo flutes and the boom boom
In the quiet sphere
With the careful caresses of the breeze
And creaking, squeaking and cracking of the trees
I will dinner with you
Cause the night is morning and morning, morning

Arikemi

I will design you on the magical arc of colours
I will wear you as a bracelet of protection
I will read you like an astrologer gapes the stars
I will live you like none lives but you
I will save you in the belly of eternity
Where worms and foes cannot trace
I will be your nerves when strength eludes you
For your love never changes, never falters, never ends

Arikemi

I will travel with you on million mountains
I will weary with you on thousand tides
I will hunger with you on deadly deserts
I will keep on with you on nucleus of nothing
I will defend you against arrows of assignation
I will tie you around my being away from storms
I will be your rays in pains, your joy in sorrow
Never to wave but stay till faith pays

You Are More

We are a knot
Too entangled to be taken apart
You are my gut
The reason I mingle in a scary path

We are too fixed
Like a gun and ammo
And too entwined
Like nothing more

You are the fireplace
The abode of my warmth
Your stare set my smirk ablaze
No words, not a single can redo or rot

You are my world
A world crafted by a word
"*let it be*", and crowned with a sword
Termed *love* – our intoxicating lord

We are on a passage

Till like Christ, after Ascension
With *'love'* our only language
Striving on, on and on with this passion

You are my existence
Won't life unquiet my fortune if each, ways?
We will wave worthy of…unless
The keeper of mortality assails

You are more, my very oar
Seeking and sticking evermore
Bearing none till I am ninety-four
When the time ticks no more

My Tender Throb…

How graceful are your smiles,
O queenly maiden!
Your round thighs are like jewels,
The artistry of a Potter
Your hip is a rounded bowl
That lacks no mixed wine
Your heart is a heap of wheat,
Encircles with blueberries
Your breasts are like two fawns,
Twins of a gazelle
Your laughter is like an Ivory tower
It reaches my distance
Your eyes are galaxies
By the gates of unguided estates
Your nose is like a tower of Burj Khalifa
Overlooking the earth
Your head crowns you like Carmel,
And your flowering looks flowing like hibiscus
Your name smells across nations,
Like your fragrance across the neighborhood

Your moaning is like a lullaby,

Clutching orchids to their tender nestles,

Your mouth is lovely with kisses like a pomegranate juice,

Indeed, like a scarlet thread

Your hug is like a shield of a warrior,

Your caress like the touch of rivers,

You have ravished my heart, *My Sunshine*!

You have ravished my soul with a glance of your eyes,

With your million romances,

Towered with butterflies in my belly

How sweet is the strength of your arms, so soft!

My being is jailed in this reverence

If...

If you are a wall,
I will build upon you a battlement of silver
a bulletproof with helmets of love
But if you are a door,
I will enclose you with sparkling boards of cedar

If you are a flower,
And I am meant to queue and pluck,
I will choose a Dahlia
Cause you are the rainbow in my cloud
But if you are not a flower,
I will conceive one and make it a chamber

If you are an ocean,
I will drown in your Pacific
Never to surface
But if you are a creek,
Let me die in the Billabong

Oh! how gracious!

If you are one of the terrestrial planets,
I will erect my heaven in the Venue
Cause your love is as red as an inferno
Let me be burnt, still, let me live

If you are a fruit,
I will give you no name
Cause the real things of life are unnamed,
I will plant you beside my bank,
Encircled with lilies
And grasped my breath from your every spring

But…
 If you are a continent,
I will call you Africa and dine in your beauty
Your colour, your nudity,
Bathed by your diverse culture
And clothe my affection with your vegetation

Oh, fairest fellow!

Turn And Sit

My Beulah!

Come and see
The wonders of your charm-
Turn and sit
And behold the awe of your arm

My Amuser!

Come and see
The galaxies your glare gathered-
Turn and sit
And behold the mountains your waists scattered

Oh! My Being!

Come and see
How inflated your twisting and scrunching and gnashing of hips have made me-
Turn and sit

And give me another anointing design
My Admiration!

Come and see
The revolution of ideas
The twinkies in my insight
Your lakes of affection have caused-
Turn and sit
And see my confessions to the globes
Of your nerves-cracking caresses

Ifemi

My name calls you *Ifemi*
This is not my mother's tongue
You treat me like *olufemi*
Like the man nailed who did no wrong

Your caress has changed my name
Even the cosmos calls me *Anyangfemi*
It is on the Earth's lips; it is written plain
Let me forever be your *Oko mi*

Tell me what I should call you, *Ifemi!*
You are the thousand rivers that erase my heart-woes
Do I call you *Ore mi?*
Even love will rive off my roofs!

Ifemi!

Tell me nothing except the journey our yearnings shall embark

For with you, I will trip far, *my Onitemi!*

To the ends of seasons to mark

Ifemi!

What shall separate me from your love?

For you are my sunrise and *Ododomi*

You worth more than sparrows and a prove

Ifemi!

You are my only *Ololufe*

Across many tribes, across million hills

You are one gold and silver coins cannot pay

Live, let's live in this castle men call cubicle

For with you, a trillion mansion I shall build

Cause you are my *Olowo ro mi,* seasons cannot wrinkle

For these promises I bind in my heart, to love along, I will

Your Love...

Your love is better than wine
Your love is comely than smile

Your love is brighter than the morning
Your love is sharper than a tungsten needle

Your love is colourful than the rainbow
Your love is sweeter than thaumatin

Your love is intoxicating than methadone
Your love is scarcer than diamond

Your love is richer than wealth
Your love is ornamental than fragrances from Lebanon

Your love is a watchman
Your love is a hope

If these are all what it is to love
I will forever be Bartimaeus

My Love Is Your Rescue

I see weapons, ice gauntlets, in your eyes
Each minute my Iris catches your iris
I see bone-chilling flames, so certain
In your eyes, agitating
At the slightest sight of me

I see again a castle, again copious castles
Clothed like a bridal center
Calling after me
With the language of your eyes

I see *need* stocked there
I see *wanting* beckoning on
I see the *yearning of me* in your soul
I see flutter of butterflies in your chuckles
Your smiles beseeching me
to answer your silence

Yet…
I see constraints in your looks
Feeling restrained like a toddler once pecked by fire

With hands of fate clutching your emotions
I see you drowning, I see me longing , I see us
And discovered that
my love
is the
only
rescue

My love
 is your
 only
rescue

Never Knew

I notice the tiny heebie-jeebies
Clutching my intestine
With drops of shivers
Making my night bone-chilling
As I sing lullabies into the quiet night

I notice my lids lie to lay
Eluding every knocking yawning
As I toss on the mattress
 like a woken baby
Impelling forty-winks to tickle my eye-wigs

I notice my grin grins at every
Drops of your winks
Making me laugh like a frantic
Teased by nothing
I notice the combat in my abdomen
The sound of cymbals in my being
I notice it is not me

I notice I call strange names

And the moon chuckled
The stars stare not in awe
Mocking my ignorance
I notice my quietness speaks
Disturbing my loneliness
Yet keeping me company

I notice I lie, principled lies
To nature
Failing to admit
I heard a call
I never knew
All the billion years
It was you

I Love Him Like That

He eats in the lagoon
And hardly gives me money for salon
I smell casual
Because he is as casual as a manual

He sleeps under bridges
He sells shoes with little or no wages
But Mama said my husband is wealth
Oh! This poverty is affecting my health!

He is Kim Taehyung
A man irreplaceably fine and strong
He gives me love
And highly treats me like a dove

He cooks like my mother
And many of these make me wonder
He apologies when I'm wrong
And apologizes when he's wrong

He has died countlessly times for me

He has built unseen future for me
He has planted my feet to sail on air
This kind is so so rare!

You may not be Dangote today
As many want their man today
I shall not define you by today
For better tomorrow shall come like ray

Cry not that I will leave you
For no wealthy man shall take me away from you
Nor will these tempests drain our love
Cause poverty will our love solve

I love him like that
It's your tea if you call him a church rat
For one man's poison is another's food
Soon, God shall make all weeds good

Journey From Hell...

...Lonely, I stood
In haste
Huffing and puffing
Like a cheetah
With multitude of unease
Crunching my bowels
While my range of view roves
Rambling, peeking and scouring
Hideously,

...Lonely, I stood
In haste
Like a retracted engine
With fat thorns hauling in rearwards
Surrounded by the Sahara.,
Trapped,
Blood streamed,
Then, I, bathed in.,

... Lonely, I stood

Hyperventilating
Like an escaped jail-bird
With moon-shades on my shoulders
With bruises in my heart
Spinning and swinging,
Unceasingly,
Slowly dragging me to the Sheol

…Lonely, I stood
Tiptoeing,
Like a cobbler's bairn without a mule
With a solemn call
Mailing nature to rescue
My surviving ashes from this ewe
Lonely, I wailed
Gnashing

Boom!

…I ran,
As brisk as a gale
Scarily,
Away, away from lethal gloves

Till dawn pecked another dawn
Till dusk pecked another dusk
Till I lost a trace
Far, far away from mortals' orb
Yet far, far away from hell
Away from your love

Then, I stalled
Suddenly,
Arrested by an embrace
An embrace, holy and inviting
As warm as a pomegranate
 Smelling like a wonderland
With sweet rustling in its smiles,
I, buried in these arms, stocked
Then, I wailed in bliss
Pledging never to go
Far, far away

A Letter To My Husband

'Eyina,
How is your day going?
Hope you slept well and have eaten?
I write to enlighten you my morning
That I am no more a kitten
Do not call me a knife

My husband, I write to inform you
To cease searching and fix your gaze here
In our house you will never desire a desert,
I am sorry for all the missiles my mouth detonated
Weep no more because of my tongue, I have worked on it
I will make my heart your lasting home
Peace shall I give like your favourite meal
Do not fret about your money, I shall be your fidelity
Are you a sex montessori? You shall never starve

See!
I shall take you to heaven

Where we last long for
I shall be a Bible – your engine room
Are you Job still? struggling to catch the sky
I will wait till this stormy sea stills

I will be your caterer
'usun' n'tutut, melek iwan-mbom
Shall grace your sight for supper
I shall be your babysitter, your teacher and your crony
You will never cry except tears of joy

I shall fight you with laughter
Murder you with courage and teachings
Forever, till eternity ceaselessly seduce you to myself alone
I will make every gutter a duplex with you
I will recreate you far beyond recognition

Reccive this missive
With courage
That in death and wealth
Hand-in-hand shall I stand

Never to wave bye
Re-read this missive
And keep pursuing your goals
Knowing that she is there
Patiently waiting and praying for you

Footnote: *usun ntutut melek iwan-mbom* means periwinkle and vegetable soup.

Tell My Love

Tell my Love I adore him
Tell him I will never again hurt him
Tell him he's my life
Tell him I will be a submissive wife

Tell my Love I apologize
For allowing wealth catch my eyes
And going after infatuations
Forgetting our predilections

Tell him I did not forget him
Tell him I wanted the best for him
That was why I left,
After unprofitable wealth

Tell my Love I have learnt
To leave him again, I can't
Love without money is abrasive
Loving him without wallet made me aggressive

How long was I to pretend

When nothing was there to lend?
How long was I to hold on
When poverty breaks my horn?

Tell him I know my wrongs
For I listened to wagging tongues
And chose a purple path
That finally tore us apart

Tell him I am back
Together to bear the mark
Of the shame
Of this broken frame

Tell him I want no more money
Cause I saw money without mind-honey
Tell him with or without wallet
I have chosen to frame him my portrait

For money without personality and felicity
Is life devoid of bliss, encompassed with difficulty
Tell him I prefer our love to those wealthy wallet
And with our love, we will control the earth

The Fire In My Choice

The lavenders have warned me of you
Did you not listen?
Even the cosmos, none left, not a few
They said I am imprisoned but a being has risen

The wind whistled war without warmth
What does it comprehend?
Loveless moth!
Come learn enchantment on my nuptial ottoman;
Your airfoils will bend!

Misery and soreness summoned me for a huddle
Storms and torrents too
Deflated my love hustle
Cause of my choice to us two

I have settled without, then within, certain
To cross Amazon with you
I have first-lined you, nothing can undo, nothing
Even after expiration, I will still choose you

The Shoot

Why are you the rhyme
That riddles my line?
Why are you so far
Yet near?
Why with you I err?
Can this be the sign
The flashes of my time?

Why are you so aged
In my heart, like the great basin bristlecone pine?
You are a kadupul – prized
A demulcent in my spine

I recall the moments
Marigolds mingle with marines
With fresh smiles accompanying,
I recall the thousand times we tarried with truth
The hard truth – never to part

Until tides timed
Until tickling feet spied

Until voices called
Until your voice gradually failed
The shoot
Boom!
And you fizzled like the dews
Waving adieu to my aches

So loud I called
So far you went
On a journey
A home
To rest
To rest alone

Dilemmas

I can cook
All
All Mama taught me
Not until I heard your voice
I wasted Mama's salt

I can wash
All
Both Adam's
Both Eve's
With a laundress's apparatuses
Not until I heard your name
I faded a white apparel

I can sing
Swing my voice
In tune to tune
Like a Canary Bird
Not until you whistled my name

My voice grew sour
And swung off-pitch
I can dance
Like the wind moves the earth
Like birds grace the spheres
Like an expectant mother after many wails
I can dance
Not until I smelt your perfume
My hips knocked like a lunatic

I am calm
Very calm
Like classical pieces
Not until I sat on your joviality
I turned a Night Club

Tell Love

Oh! My heart!
My breath capitol!
Tell love,
My earlier take
Tell her, my plight
How my life inhabited The Amazon
How my lacrimal gland homed the Pacific Ocean
How the Cardinal Points sat on my shoulders
How grief dined with me like friends

Oh! My heart!
My sacred soul!
Tell love,
My earlier take
Tell her, my plight
How death beckoned me for a kiss
Warned existence against me
How the night wrestled with the morning
To cloth me with wailings
How a second journey became a mile

Tell love,
I once gave up
Who bored my boils?
I wept gore
Drowned by anguish
Like Aissatou,
Who re-assured me?
Sorrow tossed my infant strength
Left me dazed

Oh! My Heart!
Tell love,
I loved
In the legal way
But devoured
Like a careful prey
Tell love,
My loyalty
How I never reaped
Tell her,
My never-to-love syndrome
Will she hear?

Tell her,
If she repents
If love repents
I will die
Yet again

Bedtime Canticles

Sleep well, my love, sleep well
The night visits with her youngsters,
The moon gradually strolls; while darkness chirpings
Like passerines; e-mailing another brick,
The flowers by the pathways still, like seraphs
The cold breeze of the night spreads her motherly arms
Rest well, my love, rest well.

Sleep well, my love, sleep well
My prayers are your heartbeats
For bloody feet tread the soil
With rocket-eyes and cannon paws:
Vultures, pelicans and cuckoos
Saunter with holy creeds
The night nighs sometimes with Ezekiel; sometimes with Macbeth
Some journey with the night; some awaken with her
My love is your only weapon
Rest well, my love, rest well

Poems by
Samuel Onyeche

Omalicha

(The most beautiful one)

This thing we hold is fire
dripping hot-
Like the tears of a burning nylon
Yet chill like the tongue of a stream
Like the embrace of Okara's silver Nun

Fire in the vein of water-
has this not become mystery?
Who can wholly fathom it?
Who can describe the colours
In the skin of a chameleon?

Who can number
the belly button of the sea ?
And unravel
the enigma weaved by mermaids?

Omalicham, this thing we hold
 is a garden and a grave-

A plot of ground for flowers, fruits and herbs
A six feet ditch; the interment of love,
joy and endless memories...

Obim

(My Heart Beat)

You're as pure as the finest of fountain
Endlessly flowing beside beautiful flowers
With special sparkling splash
Radiating resplendently, undying and new-
the funeral of the sun

My Angel, my dove
My Gift from above
My love for you is of comely colours
Like that of a harmless; pretty butterfly
Naturally natured in the paradise
of heavenly flowers

My heartbeat,
My daytingale, my nightingale
You are a bundle of beauteous beauty
Perfectly woven by hands, divine

You are a garland of Indian jasmine

A totem of splendor, so charming
like the lilies of Lebanon
You are that colourful smile
from the beaming cheek of a rising sun

My cocoyam; My Ubene
Though time and tide may twine
Lovely lips may lay large eggs
Of lustrous lies
In the elegant ears of harmless hearts

Though firm friends may turn foes
And like noble Brutus
Insert a stained sword
into the heart of a stainless soul

Obim, my heartbeat
Though trust may twist
And the truth may die
In the trail of time

But my love for you shall stand strong
Unshakable like the strongest of rocks

My love for you shall fresh remain
Like the fresh tempting fruits of Eden
Fluttering like the daffodils of Welshland

Scenting and scenting sweet
Like the fine fragrance
From the green garment
Of fresh Etche corn

Yes! it shall remain
sweeter and succulent
Like the urine of beautiful bees
Un-dynamic to tide nor season

My love for you
shall remain resplendent
Like the colourful wings
Of a beautiful butterfly

It shall shine as silver
No!
As gold
No!

As diamond
Yes,!

It shall steadily shine
As the skin of a virgin Diamond
Harvested from the womb of nature

Yes!
It shall steadfastly taste sweeter
Than the honeyed nectar of a petal
Happily harvested
From the veins of a Rose flower.

You Have Taught Me How To Love

You have taught me how to love
How to smile
How to sing
and how to cry
with laughter on my lips

You have taught me how to love
How to romance
the fires of the sky
How to number
the thoughts of the moon

You have taught me how to love
How to whisper
in consonants and vowels
How to swim
In tears and glee

You have taught me how to love
How to sleep

awake all night
How to dream
with open-eyes

A Home

in your sunny smile
in your lingering laughter
in your pretty shy giggle
in the beauty of your eyes

in you-
in your temporary anger
in your fragile frown
in your tears and pain
has my heart found a home

The Fire In My Lover's Skin

The miracles of the creator
Amaze me, they bend my brain
As I wonder and ponder
I often lose my head
to the wonderment of mystery

Fire and water, cold and heat
What impregnates the wombs
that gave birth to these?

Last night,
I killed cold without a duvet
The fire in my Lover's skin
keeps me warm- warmer than
the heat of the fireplace .

Fire is beautiful; a wall of defence
in the time of cold-
But the fire in your skin;
The heaven in kisses
How can I, these describe?

You Are Poetry

My love, Nwanyi-oma
Do you know you are Poetry?

I see sonnets in your eyes
Limerick on your fingers
Rhythm in your beauty
And rhymes on your teeth

Have the poets not told you
There are imagery in your smile
Litotes in your laughter
Lullabies on your lips
And paradox in your dimples?

Omalicham, you are Poetry
The aesthetics of golden Gods

I Hold Your Name

Let me smile and smile again
as I hold your name
 on my lips of laughter
I will not whisper like the wind
I will not sing like the nightingale
I will not say the words of flower
For it has been abused by many

I will just smile and smile again
Like the lips of an orange-coloured moon
Like the child in his mother's bossom
I will smile as I hold your name
on my lips of laughter
And pray that our eyes meet

Children Of Danger

Come my love

Come let us weed books

And sow seeds

In the farm of flesh

And with great glee

Anticipate huge harvest

Unlike these wily ones;

Children of danger

That sow seeds and fear harvest

The Stars In Your Eyes

When I, a writer become
I will write of the stars in your eyes
The rainbow in your smile
The moon in your laughter
And the honey on your tongue-
My pen will show the world
How beautiful true love can be

When I, a writer become
I will write of the charms in your beauty
The beauty of an angelic damsel
The damsel dancing in my head
The head shattered by the thought of love
The love of the lass in my dreams-
My pen will tell a story
A sweet story of you and I

If I Dance For You

If I dance for you ah!
If I dance for you-
You will laugh like a child
You will chortle like a child with new toy
You will forget all your troubles
You may even giggle while asleep

If I dance for you
You will scream-out oceans of laughter
You will call your neighbours to the scene
You will laugh again and again
You may even topple in joy overdose
For your neighbours will envy my steps

If I roll my Etche hands like this
And twist my garri mouth that way
Then bend down like a broken pole
Squirming my waist in slow rhythm
Forward and backward
Forward and backward like a swing

Tell me wouldn't you smile a million times?
Wouldn't your neighbours fall in love ?

If I dance for you just once
If I dance for you just once
You may break a rib or two
You may lose your teeth to laughter
Or even fall to the ground in glee
For I am a good dancer; one of a kind
But my mum says I dance like an earthworm
Even my Dad says she is right
How then can I dance for you
The dance of an earthworm

Do You Know

When I look at you
With fragile eyes

When I speak to you
In silent whispers

Do you know the
 rivers that sing within

Can you tell the
colour of the moon I see?

I Need No Cure

Olanma
Bracelet of Beauty

Omalicha
Prettiest of pearls

Onwa Olaedom
My golden Moon

You are the cause
of my madness

in this beautiful sickness
I need no cure

My Love

Each time I stare at you
A book is born.

Love And Its Pang

It is one thing to find a flower
Another...
to hold and cherish thorns.

Blessed are those
whose hands hold roses
And their eyes are not fishes-

For roses are thorns in the palm of many
Some even smile, to push down
heavy balls of sorrow-

And many cry- envying
a spurious smile
Hahaha! this chameleon
we call face has too many masks-

Let those whose *Chi* has favoured
with a palmtree
Rejoice, sing and pour thanks to earth

For it is one thing to find a flower
Another...
to hold and cherish thorns

12 Months And 11 Days

My finest; the most beautiful one
Black beauty of the morning moon.
It has been 12 months and 11 days
Since you broke the calabash and left
Thinking I would die of the cancer
The cancer only your love could cure.

Those who looked at me shaking their heads
Now stare at me with their mouths wide open
Perhaps, I have become palpable wishes
Wishes that men, women and angels admire
I have become wishes that mermaids desire.

I did not say you are the cancer, perhaps I was
But I say thank you for living when you did
For your absence has healed me of death
But for the calabash you smashed on the wall
It was not broken though it wears many scars
For true love may break, lovers may part
But the scars of love lives forever

My Wife; A Knife

My Wife is a rare queen
Tall, fair, chubby and keen
In her eye lives the earth moon
She dazzles than the sun at noon
Her beauties amaze all my clan

I am married to the most beautiful one
"She is a god among girls"I was warned
But her pulchritude wore me eyeglass
For indeed she is lustrous, a golden lass
In love and lust I dived into a grassy land

I was happy to have the most beautiful one
But there is thunder in her tiny tongue
My heart is shattered, broken and torn.
when she speaks, sharp fragments fly as thorn
Piercing ears, tearing apart our little home

I am married to the most beautiful knife
There is thunder in the tongue of my wife

When You Say You Are Sorry

Let death visit my soul now !
If I love you not-
Let heaven spit cruel curses on me
and my children unborn
If the love I profess is painted and vain

I love you- and it's you I love
I love you and you alone own my heart
You are my joy, my laughter and my peace
You are my world, my wife and my life

I have promised to stand by you
Under the sun, and in the rain
in fire of pain, In the river of tears
to fight with you, to smile with you
to reign with you, to cry with you

Yet and yet you hurt me always
Your hurt is a pain immeasurable
the bullet your tongue shoots

kills me a thousand times
yet not allowing me to die

You hurt me as death hurt a dying child
you hurt me as fire hurts a burning man
you hurt me , you hot me , you hurt me
and then you say you are sorry
When you say you are sorry

Do you think the pains go away?
Do you think the memories will ever die?
Do you think heart-wounds easily heal ?
Do you think words can heal a dying Bard?
Can a broken china be healed of Scars ?
Do you not know you have killed an only son ?

The Beauty Of A Shattered Ceramic

Some call you verbs;
the broken movement of a bad bed
But I call you my Rose flower
My beautiful first flower-
Though, our love tale
has grown cold like the beauty
of a shattered ceramic

Love Is Not For The Wise

Love is not for the Wise
Who numbers the pain of every hurt
Calculating the altitude of each wrong

Love is not for the Wise
Who writes the name of every offence
Plotting heart-graphs of red revenge

Love is not for the Wise
Whose smile holds imageries of grief
the grief of unforgiveness- that sets scars on a grave

Love is not for the Wise
Whose heart is the canvas of a calabash
 Upon which horror is etched-
horrors, holding vengeance in their hands

Love is not for the Wise
Whose heart is a bottle - like- diary

prisoner of many names, prisoner of many dark places-

 The art of witchcraft

Love is not for the Wise

Who knows the value of every grain

Always hunting to gather every gain

Never ready to loose, never willing to give

Love is for The Fool

A Bundle of Memories

Some days

You walk into my head

Into my arms

into my soul

With a bundle of memories...

When Will These Memories Go Away?

When the hen hatches its eggs
young chicks emerge-
Leaving eggs' shells behind
Eggs' shells that become birth marks
on the skin of earth.

The hen and chicks are gone
but the shells and its tale-
forever remain in the heart of earth.

Chi, you are the shells and I
the soil, holding broken memories
memories of you and I.
Chi, tell me
When will these memories go away?

Synonym Of Death

Have you ever taken sleep for dinner
And life wakes you up at midnight
To plot graphs and solve algebra of life ?
Have you slept awake all night long
Dreaming of your own funeral,composing your own graveside songs
or walked the moon into its nest with your head downwards ?

Has love ever lured you to sleep
with deep tears drenching your pillow?
Have you ever written a dirge and latter
discover it's fit for a death note ?

Have you ever made love with suicide thoughts
Or imagined the faces at your own funeral;
the faces of friends, family and foes, faking frowns?

Well, I have been my funeral planner for days now
And death is no longer scary as it used to be
perhaps, I gained the courage I once prayed for-

perhaps, I am no longer the coward of a casket
For life is a synonym of death.
My English teacher lied when she called her antonym

Nobody Can Quench This Fire

Who can stop the wind
from whispering
or scare the sun from setting ?

Has any ever held
a handful of oil in their palm
or stand against the racing of rivers ?

Who can stop the cloud from farting
Or veil heaven's eyes
 from its timely tears ?

If nobody can. If nobody has
Nobody can quench this flowers of fire
Burning with the wax of love and desire

About the Authors

Samuel Onyeche

SAMUEL ONYECHE is a Nigerian poet, whose creative works have been describe as "extraordinary". He is the Author of *Ijikrika; Canticles From Africa, On the Wings of a Butterfly* and *Parasites in Paradise and other poems*. Onyeche is a passionate writer, He holds a Bachelor's Degree in English and Literary Studies and a Masters of Art Degree in literature.

Shantel Awajionyi Igana

SHANTEL AWAJIONYI IGANA hails from Unyeada Kingdom in Andoni Local Government Area, Rivers State, Port Harcourt. She holds a Bachelor's Degree in English And Communication Art from Ignatius Ajuru University of Education, Rivers State, Port Harcourt. She is an intent writer with many beautiful works awaiting press.

www.ingramcontent.com/pod-product-compliance
Lightning Source LLC
LaVergne TN
LVHW041537070526
838199LV00046B/1699